A gift for

Manuela Perks

From

Alene Ditto, Regina Brown

Date

November 25, 2015

Under God's Umbrella

Gifts of Hope & Encouragement
to Shelter Your Heart in Life's Storms

HOLLEY GERTH

Ellie Claire
gift & paper expressions

...inspired by life

Ellie Claire® Gift & Paper Expressions
Brentwood, TN 37027
EllieClaire.com
Ellie Claire is a registered trademark of Worthy Media, Inc.

Under God's Umbrella: Gifts of Hope & Encouragement to Shelter Your Heart in Life's Storms
© 2013 by Holley Gerth
Published by Ellie Claire, an imprint of Worthy Publishing Group, a division of Worthy Media, Inc.

ISBN 978-1-60936-802-9

Writings by Holley Gerth abridged from the devotional *Rain on Me* (2008).
Compiled and edited by Joanie Garborg.

Cover and interior design by Thinkpen Design | thinkpendesign.com
Cover illustration ©2013 Shutterstock
Typesetting by Jeff Jansen | aestheticsoup.net

Printed in China

DEDICATION

FOR THE LORD
AND HIS DAUGHTERS

CONTENTS

Raindrops are splashing against the window. The storm outside looks like it will never end. Sometimes the storm in my life still feels that way too. But as I sip my mocha and stare at the sky, I know I will have God's umbrella until the sun comes out again.

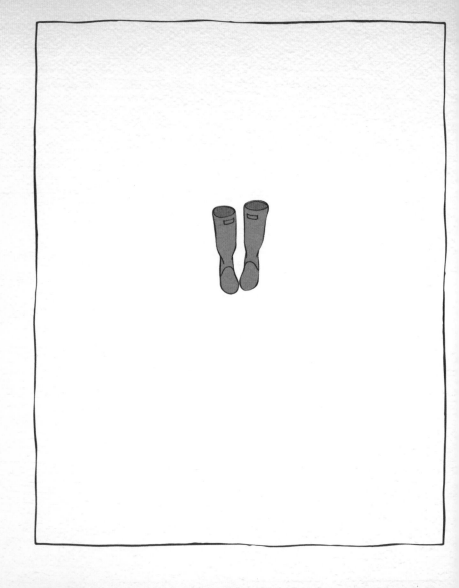

INTRODUCTION

God's umbrella has kept me from getting soaked. It has given me peace, hope, and even joy in the midst of the hardest time I've ever faced. Several years ago God allowed a storm to brew in my life that I never expected. It began as a drop, became a drizzle, and finally the heavens opened, and I found myself in an outright downpour.

After my storm began, I spent a lot of time trying to make sense of things. How could a loving God let this happen? Why wasn't He taking care of me? I still don't have the answers to all of those questions, but I no longer wonder if God loves me. I can see His hand even in this time of difficulty. I can sense Him grieving with me when I'm sad. Most of all, I have His umbrella over me, and His presence with me. There's a verse that says "His banner over me is love." I have my own version of that verse now: "His umbrella over me is love!"

I've also come to believe we don't have to wait for blue skies in order for God to use the rain that's fallen in our lives. That can start right here, right now. So wherever you are and whatever your storm may be, know that you are not alone. God is with you, and He is whispering messages about the rain to your heart that will change your world forever if you only dare to believe them. I'm praying for you as I write these words, and I'll still be praying for you as you read them.

Under God's umbrella of love with you,
Holley Gerth

Every Storm
Begins with
One Drop

*He redeems me from death and crowns me with love
and tender mercies. He fills my life with good things.*

PSALM 103:4–5 NLT

Scientists recently discovered that raindrops hit the earth at speeds of up to twenty miles an hour. Each one is like a miniature hammer pounding away dirt and scattering debris. Whether it's a small shower or a huge hurricane, raindrops make an impact. Your first drop may have been a diagnosis given by a doctor with a grim face. It could have been a phone call late at night and someone on the other end telling you the unthinkable. On the other hand, your first drop may have come so softly you didn't even recognize it. You tried to start a family and, after another negative pregnancy test, realized something might be wrong. You took a promising job and one day discovered that your computer screen might as well be a dead end sign. You began a relationship only to discover that your dream come true had started to feel a bit like a nightmare.

No matter how your first drop fell, it was probably followed by another…and another…and another. Now your heart is soaking wet and you're wondering if you'll ever feel warm and dry again. The good news is, God knows even more about rain than those scientists. He knows the destruction it can bring. He also knows how to use it to bring beauty and hope to our lives. Take a quick look out your window. Every flower or tree you see owes its life to rain. Every bird singing, every frog hopping, every living thing draws its strength from storms.

I'm not saying God caused the storm in your life. We live in a broken world, and things are not as they should be. But I do believe that God is the Redeemer of the Rain. He longs to bring beauty out of brokenness, healing out of hurts, and new life out of losses.

PRAYER

Lord, thank You for loving me and placing incredible value on each part of my life. Thank You that even the difficulties in my life can become a force that transforms loss into gain in ways I don't even fully understand. I pray that You will continue to bring healing to my life and heart. Amen.

He has sent me to bind up the brokenhearted…
to bestow on them a crown of beauty instead
of ashes, the oil of joy instead of mourning,
and a garment of praise instead of a spirit of despair.
They will be called oaks of righteousness, a planting
of the Lord for the display of his splendor.

Isaiah 61:1–3

When we focus on God, the scene changes.
He's in control of our lives; nothing lies outside
the realm of His redemptive grace.

PENELOPE J. STOKES

For you who revere my name, the sun
of righteousness will rise with healing in its rays.

MALACHI 4:2

Under that beating rain are springing up spiritual flowers
of such fragrance and beauty as never before grew....
You indeed see the rain. But do you see also the flowers?

J. M. McC., *STREAMS IN THE DESERT*

Calm me, O Lord, as You stilled the storm,
Still me, O Lord, keep me from harm.
Let all the tumult within me cease,
Enfold me, Lord, in Your peace.

CELTIC TRADITIONAL

"Don't be afraid, I've redeemed you. I've called your name. You're mine. When you're in over your head, I'll be there with you. When you're in rough waters, you will not go down. When you're between a rock and a hard place, it won't be a dead end—Because I am GOD, your personal God, The Holy of Israel, your Savior. I paid a huge price for you…! *That's* how much you mean to me! *That's* how much I love you!

ISAIAH 43:1–4 MSG

It's Okay
Not to Be Okay

I am convinced that neither death nor life, neither
angels nor demons, neither the present nor the future,
nor any powers, neither height nor depth, nor anything
else in all creation, will be able to separate us from
the love of God that is in Christ Jesus our Lord.

ROMANS 8:38–39

My grandmother has a cartoon on her refrigerator. It shows a cow on its back with all four legs in the air. The caption reads, "I'm fine, really, I'm fine." A lot of us handle the storms in our lives like that cow. We stand in the rain, soaking wet, with a smile on our faces, and say, "I'm dry, really, I'm dry."

I know what that's like because I did it for years. Somewhere along the way I was told, "Christians need to be happy all the time. If you're not happy, what will people think about Jesus?" If you want to breed a herd of perfectionists, just say that a few times from the pulpit.

For many years my life was mostly sunny. I could grin and bear it through the few showers that came along. But then came *The Storm*—the kind of storm that makes the weather channel flash maps covered with red and send warnings about taking shelter immediately.

It's one thing to stand outside in a nice little shower. It's another thing altogether to be that crazy news anchor hanging onto a light pole in the middle of a hurricane. I couldn't do it anymore.

Like the rain that streamed down in my world, something opened in my heart, and hurt poured out from a place I had kept locked for years. Then I waited. I listened for the rebukes. I watched for the disapproving stares. I stiffened my soul for the hard hand of God.

But instead of those things, I encountered the last thing I ever expected to find.

Love.

I felt it in the kindness of friends and family. I heard it in comforting words. I discovered it deep within my heart as God whispered, *I'm here with you.* I also realized I wasn't the only one who was wet. People began to open up to me. Everyone I knew had some type of rain in their lives. We were one great big beautiful, soggy mess—and God loved us all.

So if you're still muttering under your breath, "I'm dry, really, I'm dry," then I invite you to admit that there's a storm in your life. *It's okay not to be okay.*

When we embrace that grace, we're finally free to discover that love is waiting for us in the center of the storm.

PRAYER

Lord, my heart is in the midst of a storm right now.
Please help me to be honest with myself
and with You about all that I'm feeling. Amen.

God has not promised sun without rain,

joy without sorrow, peace without pain.

But God has promised strength for the day,

rest for the labor, light for the way,

grace for the trials, help from above,

unfailing sympathy, undying love.

ANNIE JOHNSON FLINT

Show the wonder of your great love....

Keep me as the apple of your eye;

hide me in the shadow of your wings.

PSALM 17:7–8

A living, loving God can and does make His presence felt,

can and does speak to us in the silence of our hearts,

can and does warm and caress us till we

no longer doubt that He is near, that He is here.

BRENNAN MANNING

God...is the end of fear; and the heart that realizes

that He is in the midst, that takes heed to the assurance

of His loving presence, will be quiet in the midst of alarm.

F. B. MEYER

God is the sunshine that warms us, the rain that melts the frost and waters the young plants. The presence of God is a climate of strong and bracing love, always there.

JOAN ARNOLD

Let your unfailing love surround us,
LORD, for our hope is in you alone.

PSALM 33: 22 NLT

Let the beloved of the LORD rest secure in him, for he shields him all day long, and the one the LORD loves rests between his shoulders.

DEUTERONOMY 33:12

Peace *with* God brings the peace *of* God. It is a peace that settles our nerves, fills our minds, floods our spirits, and in the midst of the uproar around us, gives us the assurance that everything is all right.

BOB MUMFORD

Name That Hurricane

"Don't call me Naomi," she told them. "Call me
Mara, because the Almighty has made my life
very bitter. I went away full, but the Lord *has*
brought me back empty. Why call me Naomi?"

RUTH 1:20–21

In 1953 the U.S. National Weather Service began using women's names for hurricanes. That lasted for a little over twenty years, until the women's liberation movement insisted that destructive storms be named after men too. The National Weather Service now uses six rotating lists of names that include both genders. If a storm is particularly deadly, the name is retired.

The purpose of naming a hurricane is to make it easier to track and understand. Now that you've admitted you're in a storm, I invite you to name it. Claim it as yours.

In the Bible names are powerful. When Naomi lost her husband and sons, she told people to call her Mara, which means "bitter" (Ruth 1:20). Naomi named her storm. She wanted everyone to know that raindrops of loss had fallen on her life until every last bit of hope had been washed away. Later in her story, we find that God brought hope to her again, but for this time she simply needed a way to address her pain.

What's the name of your storm? It could be loss, divorce, abuse, anger, addiction, infertility, brokenness, bankruptcy, chronic illness, death, depression, fear, guilt, or something else. Only you truly know the name your heart has spoken in the quiet moments and dark hours.

PRAYER

Lord, I'm naming my storm before You today. I give it to You and pray You'll redeem the rain in my life. Amen.

Ah, Sovereign LORD, you have made
the heavens and the earth by your great power
and outstretched arm. Nothing is too hard for you.

JEREMIAH 32:17

When life becomes all snarled up,
offer it to God and let Him untie the knots.

Then they cried out to the LORD in their trouble,
and he brought them out of their distress.
He stilled the storm to a whisper; the waves of the sea
were hushed. They were glad when it grew calm,
and he guided them to their desired haven. Let them
give thanks to the LORD for his unfailing love.

PSALM 107:28–31

Sometimes the Lord calms the storm, and other times He lets the storm rage and focuses on calming His child.

JEAN VAN DYKE

Be merciful to me, O God, be merciful to me, for in you my soul takes refuge; in the shadow of your wings I will take refuge, till the storms of destruction pass by.

PSALM 57:1 ESV

And when the storm is passed, the brightness for which He is preparing us will shine out unclouded, and it will be Himself.

MORROW COFFEY GRAHAM

His way is in the whirlwind and the storm, and clouds are the dust of his feet.

NAHUM 1:3

Even in the winter, even in the midst of the storm,
the sun is still there. Somewhere, up above the clouds,
it still shines and warms and pulls at the life buried deep
inside the brown branches and frozen earth. The sun
is there! Spring will come! The clouds cannot stay forever.

GLORIA GAITHER

Where's God When It Rains?

> *Whoever dwells in the shelter of the Most High*
> *will rest in the shadow of the Almighty.*
>
> PSALM 91:1

A few years ago, I read the book *Captivating: Unveiling the Mystery of a Woman's Soul,* by John and Stasi Eldridge. It challenges women to ask God how He's showing them His love. I was at the beginning of my storm during that time and feeling a bit abandoned, so I initially balked at the question. Finally, with a sigh, I silently asked, *Lord, how in the world are You showing me that You love me right now?*

In an instant the answer came. God spoke gently to my heart, saying, *I'm walking through the rain with you, and I'm giving you my umbrella.*

My mind flashed back to a day in college when a rainstorm swept in while I was in class. I dreaded the long trek home. As I left the classroom, I couldn't believe what I saw. My boyfriend Mark (now my husband) stood waiting for me with a smile on his face and an umbrella in his hand. He had come to walk me through the rain. It's still one of the sweetest and most loving things anyone has ever done for me.

Of course the best part of the walk home that day was staying right beside Mark. Umbrellas aren't very big, and the closer you get, the drier you stay. It's the same way with God.

I know what it's like to want to run away as fast as you can. I've done exactly that many times. However, the sweetest moments in my journey have come when I've chosen to let God wrap His loving arms around me. Being under God's umbrella isn't like a walk in the park on a sunny day. There is an intimacy to it, though, that one day we may look back on with longing.

We've all heard people say, "I'm glad that time in my life is over, but sometimes I miss how close I felt to God." God is waiting outside the door of your heart to walk you through the rain. This may not be what you would have chosen, but it will be a journey you'll always remember.

PRAYER

Lord, thank You for Your love. Sometimes it's hard to see in the midst of all this rain. I pray You will show me how You're taking care of me today. Amen.

From the ends of the earth I call to you, I call as my heart grows faint; lead me to the rock that is higher than I. For you have been my refuge, a strong tower against the foe. I long to dwell in your tent forever and take refuge in the shelter of your wings.

PSALM 61:2–4

Be strong and courageous…for it is the LORD your God
who goes with you. He will not leave you or forsake you.

DEUTERONOMY 31:6 ESV

Incredible as it may seem, God wants our companionship.
He wants to have us close to Him.
He wants to be a father to us, to shield us, to protect us,
to counsel us, and to guide us in our way through life.

BILLY GRAHAM

What do you need when circumstances puncture your fragile dikes and threaten to engulf your life with pain and confusion? You need a shelter. A listener. Someone who understands…. Do you have a place of shelter where you seek only His face? Remember it is the Lord's face you seek.

CHARLES R. SWINDOLL

He will hide me in his shelter in the day of trouble;
he will conceal me under the cover
of his tent; he will lift me high upon a rock.

PSALM 27:5 ESV

O Rock divine, O Refuge dear,
A Shelter in the time of storm.
Be Thou our Helper ever near
A Shelter in the time of storm.

VERNON J. CHARLESWORTH

How precious is your unfailing love, O God!
All humanity finds shelter in the shadow of your wings.
You feed them from the abundance of your own house,
letting them drink from your river of delights.
For you are the fountain of life, the light by which we see.

PSALM 36:7–9 NLT

In all their distress he too was distressed,

and the angel of his presence saved them.

In his love and mercy he redeemed them;

he lifted them up and carried them all the days of old.

ISAIAH 63:9

Foul-Weather
Friends

Rejoice with those who rejoice; mourn with those who mourn.

ROMANS 12:15

A few years ago my dear friend Heather faced a particularly difficult time in her life. She wrote me an e-mail pouring out her heart, speaking of the sadness she felt. I remember reading that e-mail, staring at the screen, and desperately searching for the right words with which to respond. In my mind, I probably ran through all the clichés I'd ever heard. Perhaps I even thought about a few similar experiences in my life and how those might be comforting.

In the end, however, nothing felt adequate. I didn't feel like a writer at that moment; I felt like a small, overwhelmed child searching for the right letters to form her very first sentence. So I did the only thing I knew to do. I bowed my head and asked God to fill in the blanks for me. While it doesn't often happen this way, the words below came to my heart in an instant.

> I wish I had a big yellow umbrella
>
> that would keep all the rain out of your life.
>
> I would hold it over your head,

and the drops would splash, splash,
and you would never even feel them.
But I don't have a big yellow umbrella,
so I'll walk through the rain with you.

Heather gratefully received those words and took me up on my offer. Over the next few years, we walked together through many storms. That message eventually became a greeting card.

Through that experience God showed me that we are not intended to go through our storms alone. We all need "foul-weather friends" who will venture out into the weather with us. Storms and sorrows both lose some of their strength when they are shared.

PRAYER

Lord, You didn't create us to go through life alone, especially in the hard times. I pray for friends who will walk through the rain with me. I know many of them are hurting and need someone to walk with them too. Amen.

Dear friends, let us love one another,
for love comes from God. Everyone who loves
has been born of God and knows God.

1 JOHN 4:7

Though it rains,
I won't get wet:
I'll use your love
For an umbrella.

JAPANESE FOLK SONG

Our words can promote growth by wrapping
others in a cocoon of love and hope.

GARY SMALLEY & JOHN TRENT

I pray that your love will overflow more and more,
and that you will keep on growing in
knowledge and understanding.

<small>PHILIPPIANS 1:9 NLT</small>

It is in the shelter of each other that people live.

<small>IRISH PROVERB</small>

Be of one mind. Sympathize with each other.
Love each other as brothers and sisters. Be tenderhearted,
and keep a humble attitude…. That is what God
has called you to do, and he will bless you for it.

<small>1 PETER 3:8–9 NLT</small>

"I'll cry with you," she whispered,
"until we run out of tears. Even if it's forever.
We'll do it together." There it was...a simple
promise of connection. The loving alliance
of grief and hope that blesses both our breaking
apart and our coming together again.

MOLLY FUMIA

The Beauty
of Brokenness

*This is what the L*ORD *says....*
I will pour water on the thirsty land,
and streams on the dry ground.

ISAIAH 44:2–3

There's an old story about two pots. One was perfect in every way. The other had cracks and broken places. Each day a woman filled the pots with rainwater she had collected and then carried them down the path to her home. The first pot felt proud that she never spilled a single drop. The other felt ashamed because no matter how hard she tried, she lost a lot along the way.

One day the two pots overheard the woman talking with someone who lived nearby. The neighbor exclaimed, "The flowers along your path are so beautiful! What's your secret?"

The woman answered, "One of my pots is broken, and the water that spills out helps the flowers grow every day."

We think that we have to take what's broken and make it perfect in order to be used by God and bless others. God thinks in a completely different way, however. He took what was perfect, His

Son, and made Him broken in order to bring us healing.

We're all like the second pot in the story. God sees purpose in our brokenness even when we don't, and He can use it to bring forth beauty that blesses those around us.

PRAYER

Lord, I'm so glad our brokenness can be used to produce something beautiful. I ask You to do that in my life. Please use my hurts to bring healing to others. Amen.

Let my teaching fall on you like rain; let my speech settle like dew. Let my words fall like rain on tender grass, like gentle showers on young plants.

DEUTERONOMY 32:2 NLT

When we lay the soil of our hard lives open to the rain of grace and let joy penetrate our cracked and dry places, let joy soak into our broken skin and deep crevices, *life* grows. How can this not be the best thing for the world? For us? The clouds open when we mouth thanks.

ANN VOSKAMP

God can do wonders with a broken heart
if you give Him all the pieces.

VICTOR ALFSEN

He heals the brokenhearted and binds up their wounds.
He counts the number of the stars;
He calls them all by name.

PSALM 147:3–4 NKJV

I can do all things through Christ who strengthens me.

PHILIPPIANS 4:13 NKJV

When God has become our shepherd,
our refuge, our fortress, then we can reach
out to Him in the midst of a broken world
and feel at home while still on the way.

HENRI J. M. NOUWEN

Honest to God

Then the LORD spoke to Job out of the storm.

JOB 38:1

Job is the celebrity of suffering. Most of us are very familiar with the biblical account of how God allowed Satan to take Job's children, possessions, and even health from him. After these tragedies Job sat for many days with his friends and poured out his emotions to God. His expressions included sorrow, rage, despair, frustration, and even a desire for his life to end.

Finally the Lord answers Job out of the storm. He asks Job a series of questions like "Where were you when I laid the earth's foundation?" (v. 4). At the end Job says, "My ears had heard of you but now my eyes have seen you" (42:5). What Job needed most weren't answers to his questions but rather an assurance that God was real and He was still in control despite all that had happened.

Job discovered a truth many of us never find: *Whatever it is, God can take it.* We tend to tiptoe around God as if He's a weak old man who shouldn't be upset. Or we see Him as a heavenly avenger just waiting to send yet another lightning bolt our way. But He is strong enough to handle anything we share with Him and loves us unconditionally.

If you have only been sharing with God what you think He wants to hear, then perhaps it's your turn to give full voice to your anguish and allow God the opportunity to speak to you in the storm.

PRAYER

Lord, thank You for Your unconditional love. I confess that there have been things my heart feels that I have hidden from You, and I want to bring those out into the open. Please bring Your grace and healing to this part of my life. Amen.

Conversation with the Father can be full of difficult
questions or it can be easy talking about everyday
life. It's whatever you need it to be. He is there
to listen and build a relationship with you.

Is it ok to ask the hard questions? Sure, He knows our
questions before we ask them. Is it alright to be angry
at life and at God when things don't turn out
the way we want them to? He knows that too.
Just tell Him how you feel, get it out in the open.
It's not like we can hide it from Him….

Tell God whatever you need to tell Him, ask all the
questions you want, He will never turn His back on
you. He is faithful, He is love, and He understands.

Julie Moore

Our honesty with God requires a prerequisite: honesty with ourselves.

DEBBIE GOODWIN

How long, LORD? Will you forget me forever?
How long will you hide your face from me?
How long must I wrestle with my thoughts
and day after day have sorrow in my heart?...
Look on me and answer, LORD my God....

But I trust in your unfailing love; my heart
rejoices in your salvation. I will sing the LORD's
praise, for he has been good to me.

PSALM 13:1–3, 5–6

Why do you say… "My way is hidden
from the LORD; my cause is disregarded
by my God"? Do you not know? Have you
not heard? The LORD is the everlasting God,
the Creator of the ends of the earth.
He will not grow tired or weary,
and his understanding no one can fathom.

Surrendering
Our Safety

*I have told you these things, so that in me you may
have peace. In this world you will have trouble.
But take heart! I have overcome the world.*

JOHN 16:33

We live in a world where safety is valued. We use antibacterial gel to ward off germs. We go through extensive checks at the airport. We always put railings on stairs. While we need to take precautions, there can be trouble when we transfer this way of thinking to our spiritual life. When we start believing "safety first" must be a verse in the Bible, we're headed for trouble.

There's a scene in *The Lion, the Witch and the Wardrobe*, by C. S. Lewis, when one of the children asks Mr. Beaver if the lion, Aslan, who symbolizes Christ, is safe. Mr. Beaver laughs and answers, "Who said anything about safe? 'Course he isn't safe. But he's good."

There's a vast difference between safety and security. Being safe means being protected from all hurt or injury. Being secure means knowing that no matter what happens, we'll be okay in the end.

God never promises us *safety*. We're never told that our lives will be free from storms, hurt, tragedies, or disappointments. We often quote verses like Jeremiah 29:11, which says that God has good plans for our lives. While this is definitely true, we sometimes misinterpret this message as meaning that nothing difficult will ever come our way. I was pondering this during a difficult season, and God gently whispered to my heart, *I had good plans for my Son too—but they still included a cross.*

This morning I was in a coffee shop, seated next to a group of women who were talking about "the law of attraction" and how, if you just believe, good things will come your way. They quoted Bible verses and talked about asking God for everything from men to money.

While I absolutely believe that God does answer our prayers and bring blessings, there was something missing from the conversation I overheard. There was no talk of the times when God doesn't bring us what we want. I couldn't help but wonder how these women would react when a storm blew in and their safety disappeared.

When I learned to ice skate, I was a lot like those women. I did whatever it took to never, ever fall. I inched along the ice and clung to the walls. Then one day the unthinkable happened. With a loud *smack!* my illusion of safety disappeared. But lo and behold, I survived.

That experience finally gave me the courage to get away from the wall, take some risks, and skate in a totally different way. You may be in a similar place today. You've been playing it safe. You use emotional "antibacterial gel," have extensive systems to protect your heart, and cling to the walls of life. Despite that, you are in the middle of what you tried so hard to avoid.

You have two choices: You can continue living the illusion that safety is a possibility or you can take God's hand, let Him lead you onto the ice, and begin to trust that even if you fall, He'll be there to pick you up.

PRAYER

Lord, thank You that my life is in Your hands. You are the one who offers me ultimate security no matter what happens. I release my fear to You and ask You to replace it with trust in You. Amen.

Tonight I will sleep beneath Your feet, O Lord
of the mountains and valleys, ruler of the trees and vines.
I will rest in Your love, with You protecting me
as a father protects his children, with You watching
over me as a mother watches over her children.
Then tomorrow the sun will rise and I may not know
where I am; but I know that You will guide my footsteps.

UNKNOWN

Truly my soul finds rest in God; my salvation comes
from him. Truly he is my rock and my salvation;
he is my fortress, I will never be shaken.

PSALM 62:1–2

We are ever so secure in the everlasting arms.

UNKNOWN

We serve a God who wants us to give ourselves—our
whole selves—to Him. This includes our doubts and
determinations, our fear and frustrations, our aches and
aspirations, our hollow as well as hallowed spaces.

MARGARET FEINBERG

God came to us because God wanted to join us
on the road, to listen to our story,
and to help us realize that we are not walking
in circles but moving toward the house of peace
and joy…. The God of love who gave us life
sent us [His] only Son to be with us
at all times and in all places, so that we never
have to feel lost in our struggles but always
can trust that God walks with us.

FREDERICK BUECHNER

In the beginning you laid the foundations
of the earth, and the heavens are the work
of your hands. They will perish…but you remain
the same, and your years will never end.

PSALM 102:25–27

Let the morning bring me word
of your unfailing love, for I have
put my trust in you. Show me the way
I should go, for to you I entrust my life.

PSALM 143:8

Hearts Created for Hope

We know that in all things God works for the good of those who love Him, who have been called according to His purpose.

ROMANS 8:28

God, in His infinite love, wants to help us find the potential for growth and new life hidden within each raindrop that falls in our lives. That kind of outrageous hope is the kind of hope God offers your heart today.

We were created for hope. Our bones were bred for hope. Our lungs can't breathe, our hearts won't beat, and our spirits can't thrive without it. God placed us in a world over which we have little control. And as if to compensate for this helplessness, He placed within our souls the capacity to hope—to hope for better times, to dream of better places, to pray for better outcomes, to seek better ways through life. Hope is more than optimism. Optimism is what we generate. Hope is God-given, a powerful spiritual and psychological means for transcending the circumstances.

Carrie Oliver

Hope comes from knowing that we will be in the hands of our loving heavenly Father no matter what happens. Where many would see only tragedy, we can discover the goodness of God, finding love, laughter, and the gift of life everywhere we look.

PRAYER

Lord, thank You that You are our hope and we can trust in You no matter what happens. I pray You will use the storm I am experiencing now to grow new flowers in my life in ways I never expected and help me appreciate even more the ones I've already been given. I don't fully understand yet how that is possible, but I receive Your promise to work all things together for good in my life. Amen.

God...rekindles burned-out lives with fresh hope,

Restoring dignity and respect to their lives—

a place in the sun!

1 Samuel 2:7–8 msg

Life is what we are alive to. It is not length but breadth....

Be alive to...goodness, kindness, purity, love, history,

poetry, music, flowers, stars, God, and eternal hope.

Maltbie D. Babcock

Lord, *don't hold back your tender mercies from me.*
Let your unfailing love and faithfulness always protect me.

Psalm 40:11 nlt

There will be times in life when nothing makes any sense.
All is dark. Confusion reigns. We hoped for something
great and came up empty.... But be assured that even
in this place of darkness, God is present.... Throughout
history, every great work of God started in this exact place
of emptiness.... God fills those things that are empty.

UNKNOWN

Remember your promise to me; it is my only hope.
Your promise revives me; it comforts me in all my troubles.

PSALM 119:49–50 NLT

Our hearts were made for joy. Our hearts were made
to enjoy the One who created them. Too deeply planted
to be much affected by the ups and downs
of life, this joy is a knowing and a being known by our
Creator. He sets our hearts alight with radiant joy.

WENDY MOORE

Questions
without Answers

*"For my thoughts are not your thoughts, neither
are your ways my ways," declares the L*ORD.

ISAIAH 55:8

With every drop of rain, a quiet question comes to our hearts. It's only one small word, and yet it holds our whole world within it. *Why?*

There is something within us that wants to know the reason. It seems as if understanding could somehow lessen the pain. I was part of a grief support group, and I remember the facilitator asking everyone in the room, "Do you want to know why?" Every hand was raised. Then she asked, "Would it make the hurt go away?" We all slowly shook our heads as we realized that the answers we sought wouldn't necessarily bring the healing we needed.

In *A Grief Observed*, C. S. Lewis writes about the loss of his wife. Throughout the book he wrestles with his faith. Toward the end he writes, "When I lay these questions before God, I get no answer. But a rather special sort of 'No answer.' It is not the locked door. It is more like a silent, certainly not uncompassionate, gaze. As though

He shook His head not in refusal but waiving the question. Like, 'Peace, child; you don't understand.'"

As much as we want to know, there are many things on this side of eternity that we will never understand. As a member of a book-reading club, I once read a book about the Holocaust. At one point our discussion turned to why God would allow such horrors. At the time I had recently lost my baby, and it felt as if a small holocaust had happened in my heart as well. I remember saying, "I don't know, but I feel as if God is asking me, 'Will you love Me for who you want Me to be or for who I am?'"

I don't know about you, but I want a God who doesn't allow suffering. I want a God who lets all our dreams come true, who erases death, who heals all my hurts, and who does it now. But that's not the God we serve. Somehow we have to release those expectations and decide that, despite it all, He is good, He loves us, and we love Him.

One of my heroes, Angie Smith, wrote in her blog, *Bring the Rain*, about the loss of her daughter Audrey Caroline and compared it to Moses' mother releasing her son in a basket onto the river:

Sometimes I think it's harder to believe the way I do, because I believe with everything in me that He could have changed the story. This line of thinking inevitably brings me to the question, "Why didn't He?" Many people have written me with the same question, and I want to tell you that I have thought it through many times, and I have come up with a great theological explanation that I want to share with you.

I have absolutely no idea.

What I do know is this: The Lord walks beside me as He walked beside Moses, and He knows me by name. He loves me, and I love Him. I pushed my baby through the reeds and never saw her again. And yet here I am, worshipping the God who allowed it.

Angie Smith

At some point, we all come to the place where we're asked to open our hands, release our questions, and embrace the One whose ways we do not understand but whose heart we know. And the moment we can finally trade our "why" for a "Who," the rest of our journey changes.

PRAYER

Lord, I have many questions without answers.
I want to know why storms happen in my life.
But even more than that, I want to know Your heart.
So I release my questions to You. Even if they
are never answered this side of eternity,
I will still love and trust You. Amen.

Everything God does is love—
even when we do not understand Him.

<small>UNKNOWN</small>

*You will keep in perfect peace those whose minds
are steadfast, because they trust in you.
Trust in the LORD forever, for the LORD,
the LORD himself, is the Rock eternal.*

<small>ISAIAH 26:3–4</small>

Faith helps us to live with the unanswered.
Hope helps us to live with the unresolved. Trust helps
us to accept…and go on with the work of living.

<small>MARK CONNOLLY</small>

Trust in the LORD with all your heart and lean not
on your own understanding; in all your ways submit
to him, and he will make your paths straight.

PROVERBS 3:5–6

Faith is deliberate confidence in the character of God
whose ways you may not understand at the time.

OSWALD CHAMBERS

The LORD is like a father to his children,
tender and compassionate to those who fear him.
For he knows how weak we are; he remembers
we are only dust. Our days on earth are like grass;
like wildflowers, we bloom and die. The wind blows,
and we are gone—as though we had never been here.
But the love of the LORD remains forever.

PSALM 103:13–17 NLT

I know that God is faithful. I know that He answers

prayers, many times in ways I may not understand.

The "Yes"
You Never Expected

He stilled the storm to a whisper;
the waves of the sea were hushed.

PSALM 107:29

A few years ago, a coworker came rushing up to my desk with good news to share. She exclaimed, "A greeting card you wrote has been nominated for an award!" I asked her what kind of card it was, and she replied, "Baby congratulations."

After she walked away from my desk, I sat in stunned silence for a few moments as I considered the irony. An infertile woman might receive an award for a baby congratulations card! As I looked back over the past few years, several other similar instances came to mind. I unexpectedly got to help develop a line of baby gifts. I published three books for children.

Slowly the Lord began to reveal something to my heart. I sensed Him softly whispering, *I've said yes to every prayer that has been prayed for new life to come through you. It has just been in a different way than you expected.*

As I absorbed those words, tears came to my eyes. I knew it was true. I also knew that I had believed a lie. That lie went something like, "You did something wrong, and so God is saying no to your prayers." I thought if I could just be better, then somehow I could earn what I wanted.

Now, though, I suddenly realized God had been saying yes all along. In that moment God "stilled the storm to a whisper" in my life. Before then all I could hear was the rain pounding against my heart, and the steady beat sounded like *no, no, no, no.*

You've heard that sound, haven't you? Late at night, when all is quiet. In the middle of the day, when you're caught off guard by a painful longing or unwelcome memory. In the morning, when you wake up to another day when things are not as they should be.

Yet if we listen closer, there is another sound. It's the heartbeat of our heavenly Father saying *yes, yes, yes, yes.* Even when we don't understand, *yes.* Even when it's different than what we expected, *yes.* Even when it seems as if nothing good is happening, *yes.*

Over the next few months, five people told me on separate occasions that they felt God was going to bring new life through my words. I hadn't told any of them what God had revealed to my heart, and it was further confirmation of what I'd sensed to be true. Not having a child still hurt, but I also found renewed peace in knowing that God was at work.

Perhaps it's time for you to ask your heavenly Father to "still the storm to a whisper" in your life and help you hear His voice in a new way. You just may discover a *no* in your life is actually a *yes* you never expected.

PRAYER

Lord, sometimes it's hard to tell when You are saying yes *because what You're doing looks and feels so much like a* no *to me. I pray You'll help me to see how You may be answering in ways I didn't expect. Speak to me in a new way today. Amen.*

Open wide the windows of our spirits
and fill us full of light; open wide the door
of our hearts that we may receive and entertain
Thee with all the powers of our adoration.

CHRISTINA ROSSETTI

God is always at work around us. He wants to
involve us in what He is already doing.

ALLEN WHITE

The LORD will work out his plans for my life—
for your faithful love, O LORD, endures forever.
Don't abandon me, for you made me.

PSALM 138:8 NLT

*You know with all your heart and soul that not one
of all the good promises the LORD your God gave
you has failed. Every promise has been fulfilled.*

JOSHUA 23:14

When God shuts a door, He opens a window.

JOHN RUSKIN

When one door…closes another opens; but often
we look so long at the closed door that we do not
see the one which has been opened for us.

HELEN KELLER

God may not provide us with a perfectly ordered
life, but what He does provide is Himself, His
presence, and open doors that bring us closer
to being productive, positive, and realistic.

JUDITH BRILES

He is the Rock, his works are perfect, and all
his ways are just. A faithful God who does
no wrong, upright and just is he.

DEUTERONOMY 32:4

We shall come one day to a heaven
where we shall gratefully know that
God's great refusals were sometimes
the true answers to our truest prayer.

P. T. FORSYTH

Singing in the Rain

I will sing to the LORD, for he is highly
exalted.... He has become my salvation.

EXODUS 15:1–2

It's one thing to look back on the storm and praise God; it's quite another to raise your hands to heaven when the lightning is flashing and the thunder is roaring. It's only through the amazing grace of God that we can do so. Rather than the storm drowning out our voices, the praise we give God during difficult times is the most audible of all to the world.

The songs the world hears from our hearts are also for our healing. God desires our praises, but He doesn't need them. However, He knows that *we* do. In the deepest, darkest moments of our lives, we need to affirm what is true: We are loved, there is a greater plan, and God is still in control. The words we lift to heaven also lift our hearts from despair. We're all called to sing in the rain. When we do so, our Heavenly Father hears every word, the world takes notice, and our hearts are never the same.

PRAYER

Lord, I choose to glorify You today regardless of how I feel. May the words of my heart touch Yours and be used to make a difference in the lives of those around me. Amen.

Let all who take refuge in you be glad; let them ever
sing for joy. Spread your protection over them,
that those who love your name may rejoice in you.

PSALM 5:11

I have lived pain and my life can tell: I only deepen the
wound of the world when I neglect to give thanks for early
light dappled through leaves and the heavy perfume of
peonies in June and the song of crickets on summer humid
nights and the rivers that run and the stars that rise and the
rain that falls and all the good things that a good God gives.

ANN VOSKAMP

*Satisfy us in the morning with your unfailing love,
that we may sing for joy and be glad all our days.*

PSALM 90:14

How much greater is my peace when I find it has come in
the midst of the storm and not because He stilled its forces.

LEITA TWYEFFORT

You will go out in joy and be led forth in peace;
the mountains and hills will burst into song before you,
and all the trees of the field will clap their hands.

ISAIAH 55:12

Let us give all that lies within us...to pure praise,
to pure loving adoration, and to worship from
a grateful heart—a heart that is trained to look up.

AMY CARMICHAEL

Watch how the trees exult when the wind is in them.

Mark the utter stillness of the great blue heron

in the swamp. Listen to the sound of the rain.

Learn how to say Hallelujah from the ones who say it.

FREDERICK BUECHNER

Holding
onto Hope

Let us hold unswervingly to the hope we
profess, for he who promised is faithful.

HEBREWS 10:23

J wear two rings. The ring on my left hand represents the commitment I've made to my husband.

The one on my right hand is a simple silver band with the word *Hope* inscribed on it. After experiencing a difficult season in my life, I bought the ring to be a daily reminder of my commitment to God and myself to live in hope no matter what happens.

Before this time in my life, I thought hope was an emotion. Now, though, I've realized it's so much more. I wrote about that in a greeting card for which I created the message:

> Hope is more than a word—it's a state of being.
> It's a firm belief that even if you don't know how,
> even if you don't know when, God will come through
> and better days are ahead. Life brings rain…
> Hope dances in the puddles Until the sun comes out again.

Hope comes from perseverance and a stubborn belief that God is faithful even when the evidence suggests the contrary.

There are many times when hope seems to be gone. That's why it's important to make a conscious commitment to living in hope rather than relying on emotions. My ring is a visible reminder of that truth.

The world or our circumstances may tell us, "Hope is dead. On those days we have to remember that we're committed to hope no matter what happens. Even when we can't see it. Even when we don't feel it. Even when all evidence suggests the opposite.

Committing to hope doesn't mean believing that one day we'll get what we want. True hope is believing in unchanging truths: that God is good, He has a plan, and we are loved. Like a strong marriage, that kind of hope can see us through a lifetime of "for better or for worse."

PRAYER

Lord, I thank You that You are the "God of hope." Please renew my hope and help me to commit to living in hope for a lifetime, no matter what happens. Amen.

When the world says, "Give up,"
Hope whispers, "Try it one more time."

Hope is not only the light you carry within,
it is also what often carries you through.

Unknown

Show me your ways, Lord, teach me your paths. Guide
me in your truth and teach me, for you are God my Savior,
and my hope is in you all day long. Remember, Lord,
your great mercy and love, for they are from of old.

Psalm 25:4–6

God shall be my hope, my stay, my
guide and lantern to my feet.

Shakespeare

May the God of hope fill you with all joy and peace as you trust in him, so that you may overflow with hope.

ROMANS 15:13

In the presence of hope—faith is born. In the presence of faith—love becomes a possibility! In the presence of love—miracles happen!

DR. ROBERT SCHULLER

Those who hope in the LORD will renew their strength. They will soar on wings like eagles; they will run and not grow weary, they will walk and not be faint.

ISAIAH 40:31

Faith means being sure of what we hope for...now.

It means knowing something is real, this moment,

all around you, even when you don't see it.… It's simply

taking God at His word and taking the next step.

Joni Eareckson Tada

Make Every
Day Count

Teach us to number our days, that we
may gain a heart of wisdom.

PSALM 90:12

Sometimes the rain in our lives blinds us to everything else. Yet even in those moments, there are still beauty, joy, and blessings to uncover. We can embrace the good along with the bad during challenging seasons.

Recently I'd been through several losses and felt utterly discouraged. One day I prayed, *Lord, I feel like I'm in a deep, dark cave right now.* Of course I didn't hear an audible response, but He did impress on my heart, *You may be in a cave, but you have a choice: You can sit in the dark, or you can diamond-mine your difficulties.*

I decided then and there that I wasn't leaving that cave in my life empty-handed. I was going to take every blessing I could find with me. There were still many days when all I did was sit on the floor of the cave and grieve, but I also walked away from that time in my life with treasures I would never have found otherwise.

PRAYER

Lord, thank You that each day of my life belongs to You. I pray that You will help me make this day count. Whatever I go through, redeem it and use it for Your purposes. Amen.

Taken separately, the experiences of life can work harm and not good. Taken together, they make a pattern of blessing and strength the like of which the world does not know.

V. RAYMOND EDMAN

Though the fig tree does not bud and there are no grapes on the vines, though the olive crop fails and the fields produce no food, though there are no sheep in the pen and no cattle in the stalls, yet I will rejoice in the LORD, I will be joyful in God my Savior.

HABAKKUK 3:17–18

In difficulties, I can drink freely of God's power and experience His touch of refreshment and blessing— much like an invigorating early spring rain.

ANABEL GILLHAM

When life gets really difficult, don't jump to the conclusion
that God isn't on the job…. This is a spiritual refining
process, with glory just around the corner.

1 PETER 4:12–13 MSG

*God will not permit any troubles to come upon
us, unless He has a specific plan by which great
blessing can come out of the difficulty.*

PETER MARSHALL

Be truly glad. There is wonderful joy ahead,
even though you have to endure many trials for a little
while. These trials will show that your faith is genuine.
It is being tested as fire tests and purifies gold—
though your faith is far more precious than mere gold.

1 PETER 1:6–7 NLT

Each day is a treasure box of gifts from God,

just waiting to be opened.

Open your gifts with excitement....

You will find love wrapped in sparkling gems.

Joan Clayton

Last on the List

Suffering produces perseverance; perseverance,
character; and character, hope.

ROMANS 5:3–4

When I first read the verse above, I wondered if my Bible had a typo. Wasn't hope supposed to be at the beginning of the list? That's certainly where I wanted it to be. I didn't like the idea of going through suffering, perseverance, and character to get to hope. But this passage makes it clear that hope is a *process*.

As Dwight L. Moody said, "Character is what you are in the dark." Character also becomes a light in the dark because it eventually results in hope. This kind of hope is not a vague feeling or wish. Instead it's a deep knowledge that you and God can get through anything together.

That's the heart of hope: choosing to walk with God through the valleys of life and finding that He will never leave you—and that you will never leave Him either.

PRAYER

Lord, I pray You will meet me in the midst of my suffering today and help me to persevere. May this difficulty transform who I am, the very essence of my character. Thank You for the hope You give me. Amen.

Look back from where we have come.

The path was at times an open road of joy,

At others a steep and bitter track of stones and pain.

How could we know the joy without the suffering?

And how could we endure the suffering but that

we are warmed and carried on the breast of God?

DESMOND M. TUTU

If suffering went out of life, courage, tenderness, pity, faith, patience, and love in its divinity would go out of life, too.

FATHER ANDREW SDC

Hope that is seen is not hope; for why does one still hope for what he sees? But if we hope for what we do not see, we eagerly wait for it with perseverance.

ROMANS 8:24–25 NKJV

Character cannot be developed in ease and quiet. Only through experience of trial and suffering can the soul be strengthened, vision cleared, ambition inspired, and success achieved.

HELEN KELLER

You, LORD, keep my lamp burning; my God turns my darkness into light.

PSALM 18:28

God possesses infinite knowledge and an awareness which is uniquely His. At all times, even in the midst of any type of suffering, I can realize that He knows, loves, watches, understands, and more than that, He has a purpose…. Comfort and prosperity have never enriched the world as adversity has done. Out of pain and problems have come the sweetest songs, the most poignant poems, the most gripping stories. Out of suffering and tears have come the greatest spirits and the most blessed lives.

BILLY GRAHAM

I am always with you; you hold me by my right hand. You guide me with your counsel, and afterward you will take me into glory. Whom have I in heaven but you? And earth has nothing I desire besides you.

PSALM 73:23–25

Praise be to the God and Father of our Lord Jesus Christ, the Father of compassion and the God of all comfort, who comforts us in all our troubles.

2 CORINTHIANS 1:3–4

Wherever you are today, whatever you are questioning, there are some things that will always be true. The God who has seen the brokenness still calls you His own and still loves you. He doesn't want you to run away but rather to run into His arms, to find the healing your heart so desperately needs.

PRAYER

Lord, thank You that even when I run away, You pursue my heart and never let me go. Please show me Your love today in the midst of my hurt. Amen.

Why would God promise a refuge unless He knew
we would need a place to hide once in a while?

NEVA COYLE

The eternal God is your refuge, and
underneath are the everlasting arms.

DEUTERONOMY 33:27

*God walks with us…. He scoops us up in
His arms or simply sits with us in silent
strength until we cannot avoid the awesome
recognition that yes, even now, He is here.*

GLORIA GAITHER

"You will seek me and find me when you seek me with all
your heart. I will be found by you," declares the LORD.

JEREMIAH 29:13–14

When a baffling or painful experience comes,
the crucial thing is not always to find the right
answers, but to ask the right questions....
To refuse to ask honest questions of ourselves
ultimately means shutting ourselves off from revelation.
Often it is simply the right question at the right time
that propels us on into the journey of awakening.

SUE MONK KIDD

My Presence will go with you,
and I will give you rest.

EXODUS 33:14

From the tiny birds of the air and from the fragile lilies
of the field we learn the same truth.... God takes care
of His own. He knows our needs. He anticipates our crises.
He is moved by our weaknesses. He stands ready to come
to our rescue. And at just the right moment He steps
in and proves Himself as our faithful heavenly Father.

Share Rather
than Compare

Carry each other's burdens, and in this way
you will fulfill the law of Christ.

Galatians 6:2

The raindrops that fall on us are the ones that soak our souls—even if we're only in a thunderstorm and someone we know is in a category 5 hurricane. We need to give ourselves permission to stop comparing our pain to that of others. It's okay to embrace that our hurt is real, legitimate, and worthy of our tears.

As we do, we'll be able to stop comparing and instead start sharing. We don't need to experience everything in order to have compassion. Even if we did go through the same thing as someone else, our journey would be different. Instead we can say, "Your pain is not more or less significant than mine. What matters is that I know what it's like to hurt, and I will hurt with you." When we share rather than compare, we lighten the weight of grief both for those around us and for ourselves because we truly begin to carry each other's burdens.

PRAYER

Lord, I'm so glad You look at us individually rather than comparing us to each other. Help me to do the same. I choose to own and acknowledge my hurt rather than denying or diminishing it. Amen.

In good times and bad, we need friends who will
pray for us, listen to us, and lend a comforting
hand and an understanding ear when needed.

BEVERLY LaHAYE

Love makes burdens lighter, because you divide them.
It makes joys more intense, because you share them.
It makes you stronger, so that you can
reach out and become involved with life
in ways you dared not risk alone.

UNKNOWN

Clothe yourselves with compassion, kindness,
humility, gentleness and patience. Bear with each
other…. And over all these virtues put on love,
which binds them all together in perfect unity.

COLOSSIANS 3:12–14

We are truly loving when we help ourselves and others
to be all we are meant to be. A loving life is a life where
there is a balance between fulfilling our own needs
and caring enough about others to help them fulfill theirs.

ALEXANDRA STODDARD

Let's not get tired of doing what is good.
At just the right time we will reap a harvest of blessing
if we don't give up. Therefore, whenever we have
the opportunity, we should do good to everyone.

GALATIANS 6:9–10 NLT

It is in identifying yourself with the hopes,
dreams, fears, and longings of others that you
may understand them and help them.

WILFERD A. PETERSON

God give me joy in the common things:
In the dawn that lures, the eve that sings....
In the thought that life has love to spend,
In the faith that God's at journey's end.
God give me hope for each day that springs,
God give me joy in the common things!

THOMAS CURTIS CLARK

PRAYER

Lord, You know that I want You to remove this difficulty from my life. I've asked You to do so many times. But today I'm coming to ask You to show me how You want to use this situation in my life for Your purposes. I wouldn't have chosen this, but I do believe that You can make something good come from it. You waste nothing in our lives, including our hurts. I pray You will take the healing You have done in my life and show me how I can use it to help others. Please help me to be an encouragement in their lives. Amen.

Bring your soul to the Great Physician—exactly
as you are…. For it is in such moments that you
will most readily sense His healing presence.

St. Teresa of Avila

Why are you in despair, O my soul? And why have you
become disturbed within me? Hope in God, for I shall again
praise Him for the help of His presence…. The Lord will
command His lovingkindness in the daytime; and His song
will be with me in the night, a prayer to the God of my life.

Psalm 42:5–8 nasb

God makes our lives a medley of joy and tears,
hope and help, love and encouragement.

Give, and it will be given to you. A good measure,
pressed down, shaken together and running over,
will be poured into your lap. For with
the measure you use, it will be measured to you.

LUKE 6:38

God wants us to lay our burdens on Him and rest
in His love. It's His responsibility to work out
the purpose and plan in our hardships. Only our refusal
to trust Him...can hinder His purposes in our lives.

JONI EARECKSON TADA

Most of all, love each other as if your life depended on it.
Love makes up for practically anything....
Be generous with the different things God gave you.

1 PETER 4:8, 10 MSG

Can we find a friend so faithful,

Who will all our sorrows share?

Jesus knows our every weakness:

Take it to the Lord in prayer.

JOSEPH M. SCRIVEN

The Center
of the Storm

You make known to me the path of life;

you will fill me with joy in your presence,

with eternal pleasures at your right hand.

PSALM 16:11

God's presence is the eye of the storm, the place where we can find calm in the midst of all that's happening around us. We can be in the midst of a storm and still be okay because He is there. His presence makes all the difference. That's why it's so vital to set aside time each day to spend with Him.

While God is always with us, there's something special about those moments when we pull away from everything else and have time alone with Him. His presence is a safe place for our hearts.

When we take time to be with God—especially when things are difficult—we rediscover that it's not where we are in life but who is with us that truly makes all the difference.

PRAYER

Lord, I want to live daily in Your presence. Help me to be disciplined and make spending time with You a priority. Help me to deal with those things that make it harder for me to connect with You. Amen.

Entering that rest—choosing God
as our resting place—is more about
our hearts and less about our hands.
It's what's going on inside far more
than what is going on outside.
Rest is an internal state of soul,
a relaxing into God's chest even when
dashing through a day or season.

JANE RUBIETTA

In returning and rest you shall be saved;

in quietness and confidence shall be your strength.

ISAIAH 30:15 NKJV

You have made us for Yourself, O Lord,
and our heart is restless until it rests in You.

AUGUSTINE

The LORD is my shepherd; I shall not want.

He makes me to lie down in green pastures;

He leads me beside the still waters. He restores my soul….

Surely goodness and mercy shall follow me

all the days of my life; and I will dwell

in the house of the LORD Forever.

PSALM 23:1–6 NKJV

God is as near as a whispered prayer

No matter the time or place…

In His mercy and great compassion

He will ease, He will help, He will share!

Whatever your lot,

Take heart in the thought:

God's as near as a whispered prayer!

JON GILBERT

Rest in the LORD, and wait patiently for him.

PSALM 37:7 KJV

Those who run in the path of God's
commands have their hearts set free.

UNKNOWN

It's good to pause sometimes and look back over how far you've come. In which areas of your life have you been freed with God's help? What steps will you take to ensure you continue to live in freedom and hope?

Embracing the freedom that we have worked to gain doesn't mean we won't hurt, have setbacks, or struggle again. It does mean that we choose to take what God has done in us and live it out. That requires courage, determination, and resilience.

While we have to fight hard to get and stay free, God is the One who makes it possible. The key to moving forward in freedom is walking with Him, rain or shine, every step of the way.

PRAYER

Lord, thank You for all You have done
in my life and heart. I ask that You will help me
to continue the changes You have begun in me.
Teach me to live in freedom. Amen.

Grasp the fact that God is for you—let this certainty make its impact on you in relation to what you are up against at this very moment; and you will find in thus knowing God as your sovereign protector, irrevocably committed to you in the covenant of grace, both freedom from fear and new strength for the fight.

J. I. PACKER

If God is for us, who can be against us?

ROMANS 8:31

In almost everything that touches our everyday life on earth, God is pleased when we're pleased. He wills that we be as free as birds to soar and sing our maker's praise.

A. W. TOZER

Bruised Reeds
and
Smoldering Wicks

A bruised reed He will not break,

and a smoldering wick He will not snuff out.

God says to each of us: *I will meet you in your weakness, and I will not press you down. Instead I will lift you up with love.*

Our Lord is like a protective shepherd. When a member of a shepherd's flock is hurt, the shepherd rescues that animal, tends to its wounds, keeps it close by his side to protect it from further harm, and even carries it on his shoulders. A shepherd sees weakness as an opportunity for loving care.

Close your eyes for a moment and hear Him speak to your wounded heart: *"My child, you are a bruised reed, and I will not crush you. You are a smoldering wick, and I will not snuff you out."*

PRAYER

Lord, I feel especially vulnerable during this time of my life. I ask for You to protect me, to strengthen me, and to gently lift me up with Your love. Amen.

God is the shepherd in search of His lamb.

His legs are scratched, His feet are sore,

and His eyes are burning. He scales the cliffs

and traverses the fields. He explores the caves.

He cups His hands to His mouth and calls into

the canyon. And the name He calls is yours.

MAX LUCADO

When God has become our shepherd, our refuge, our
fortress, then we can reach out to Him in the midst of a
broken world and feel at home while still on the way.

HENRI J. M. NOUWEN

*He shall gather the lambs with His arm,
and carry them in His bosom.*

ISAIAH 40:11 KJV

My Good Shepherd, who has shown Your very
gentle mercy to us,...give grace and strength to
me, Your little lamb, that in no tribulation or
anguish or pain may I turn away from You.

ST. FRANCIS OF ASSISI

Here is perfect safety: in His bosom who can
hurt us? They must hurt the Shepherd first.
Here is perfect rest and sweetest comfort.

CHARLES H. SPURGEON

He won't brush aside the bruised and the hurt
and he won't disregard the small and insignificant,
but he'll steadily and firmly set things right.

ISAIAH 42:3 MSG

Your Savior knows your breaking point.
The bruising and crushing and melting process
is designed to reshape you, not ruin you. Your value
is increasing the longer He lingers over you.

CHARLES R. SWINDOLL

The Last Tear

Record my misery; list my tears on your scroll—

are they not in your record?

PSALM 56:8

God truly is the only one who can wipe every tear from our eyes, and one day He will. The story of our loss can only be completed in eternity. While we may not understand it, God is still writing each word with love. He promises to give us strength, peace, and hope for each page. His Son died for us so that our sorrows could be healed and we could be in a place without pain forever. Christ's final words on the cross were "It is finished." And on the day He wipes away the last tear from our eyes, those will be the closing words in the story of our heartaches as well.

PRAYER

Lord, I know that one day You will wipe away every tear from my eyes. Until that time, I need Your help to make it through this journey. Thank You for walking with me today. Amen.

They will be his people, and God himself
will be with them and be their God.
He will wipe every tear from their eyes.
There will be no more death or mourning
or crying or pain, for the old order
of things has passed away.

REVELATION 21:3–4

God writes with a pen that never blots, speaks with a tongue
that never slips, and acts with a hand that never fails.

HUBERT VAN ZELLER

GOD rewrote the text of my life when
I opened the book of my heart to his eyes.

PSALM 18: 24 MSG

*The story of your life will be the story
of prayer and answers to prayer.*

OLE HALLESBY

God loves you in the morning sun and the evening

rain, without caution or regret…. God loves

without condition or reservation, and loves you this

moment as you are and not as you should be.

BRENNAN MANNING

The LORD is gracious and full of compassion…. The LORD

is good to all, and His tender mercies are over all His works.

PSALM 145:8–9 NKJV

We can be assured of this: God, who knows all

and sees all, will set all things straight in the end.

Even better, He will dry every tear. In the meantime

He mysteriously takes our sorrows and uses them.

RICHARD J. FOSTER

Your Companion
for the Journey

He will give you another Counselor to be
with you forever—the Spirit of truth…
You know Him, for He lives with you and will be in you.

<small>JOHN 14:16–17</small>

Dick and Rick Hoyt have competed in dozens of marathons and numerous triathlons as a father-son team. What makes this pair so unusual is that Rick has severe cerebral palsy and can't walk or talk. He has learned to communicate using a special computer. Doctors encouraged the Hoyts to place their son in a home. However, Dick and his wife were determined to raise him like any other child.

At age fifteen Rick asked his father to push him in a wheelchair so he could be part of a race raising money for charity. Although they finished second to last, the race felt like a triumph. Rick told his father he "didn't feel handicapped" when they were competing. Twenty-five years and over eighty marathons and eight triathlons later, Team Hoyt is still going strong. For Dick, now over sixty-five, this process hasn't been easy. The competitions are physically challenging, as well as mentally and emotionally draining. Nevertheless, for Dick every minute of exertion and every mile of endurance is worth it.

Imagine if we each had someone like him who would run the race of life with us—someone who would do for us what we could never do for ourselves, who would see our inherent value and love us just as we are, who would take us all the way to the finish line. Jesus told us that we do have someone just like that in our lives and hearts. He told His disciples, "I will ask the Father, and He will give you another Counselor to be with you forever—the Spirit of truth" (John 14:16–17).

For many of us, the Holy Spirit is the most mysterious member of the Trinity. But understanding His role is vital to living fully, especially during difficult times. The Holy Spirit comforts, empowers, and leads us. He speaks truth to our hearts when we need it most. Like Dick Hoyt with his son, the Holy Spirit does in and through us what we could never do for ourselves.

If Rick looked for his father during a race, he probably wouldn't be able to see him. That's because Dick is always behind his son, exerting all of his energy to move him forward. But Rick can feel the wheels of his chair turning, he can hear the encouraging words being spoken to him, he can see the finish line drawing closer and closer.

In much the same way, we can trust that the Holy Spirit is always with us. As we rely completely on Him, He'll work on our behalf, guide us with love, and ensure we're triumphant no matter what we may face.

PRAYER

Holy Spirit, I'm so glad You're always with me. Thank You for being my comforter, counselor, encourager, and guide. Help me know and understand You better. Amen.

God is nothing if not personal....
Father, Son, and Holy Spirit;
God-in-community—
we are given an understanding
of God that is emphatically personal.
The only way He reveals Himself
or works among us is personal.

EUGENE PETERSON

In God's love, He is fully able to guide you through the special plans He has for your life.

Where can I go from your Spirit? Where can I flee from your presence? If I go up to the heavens, you are there; if I make my bed in the depths, you are there. If I rise on the wings of the dawn, if I settle on the far side of the sea, even there your hand will guide me, your right hand will hold me fast.

PSALM 139:7–10

We have ample evidence that the Lord is able to guide. The promises cover every imaginable situation. All we need to do is to take the hand He stretches out.

ELISABETH ELLIOT

Heaven often seems distant and unknown,
but if He who made the road...is our guide,
we need not fear to lose the way.

HENRY VAN DYKE

Create in me a pure heart, O God, and renew a steadfast
spirit within me. Do not cast me from your presence
or take your Holy Spirit from me. Restore to me the joy
of your salvation and grant me a willing spirit, to sustain me.

PSALM 51:10-12

*Our Father, sometimes You seem so far away,
as if You are a God in hiding.... At times when we
feel forsaken, may we know the presence of the Holy
Spirit who brings comfort to all human hearts.*

PETER MARSHALL

Christian hope,

unlike most other kinds of hope,

is not mere optimism. It's not even a matter

of thinking positively: "Cheer up.

Things will work." Christian hope

is applied faith. If God Himself is here

with us in His Holy Spirit,

then all things are possible.

BRUCE LARSON

Beyond
the Rain

When the dove returned to him in the evening,
there in its beak was a freshly plucked olive leaf!
Then Noah knew that the water had receded from the earth.

GENESIS 8:11

My heart's desire is that you've come to believe in a deeper way that, while God may not cause the rain in our lives, He's committed to redeeming every drop. He wants to use it to quench our thirsty souls, bring forth life from the barren desert of our hearts, and grow a garden of blessings filled with a beauty we never imagined possible in the midst of our pain.

Rain is inevitable; hope and resilience are optional. But with God's help, both can be ours no matter what we may face.

PRAYER

Lord, please continue to use the storms in my life to bring new growth, healing, and hope to my heart. Amen.

Go forth
with an umbrella of love,
a heart full of grace,
and a determination
to never stop
until God redeems
each raindrop in your life
and you receive every
olive leaf of hope
our heavenly Father has for you.

*H*olley Gerth is a best-selling writer, licensed counselor, certified life coach, and speaker. She is cofounder of (in)courage, an online destination for women, which received more than one million page views in its first six months. She also reaches out to readers through her popular blog, Heart to Heart with Holley and through a partnership with DaySpring. She is passionate about bringing hope to the hearts of women and continues to find creative new ways to do so. Holley lives in the South with her husband, Mark. You can connect with Holley online at www.holleygerth.com